EVERYTHING YOU MUST KNOW ABOUT RADIOACTIVITY 6TH GRADE CHEMISTRY

Children's Chemistry Books

BABY PROFESSOR

EDUCATION KIDS

In this book, we're going to cover the different types of radioactivity. So, let's get right to it!

In order to understand radioactivity, you need to know a little about elements and their atomic structure.

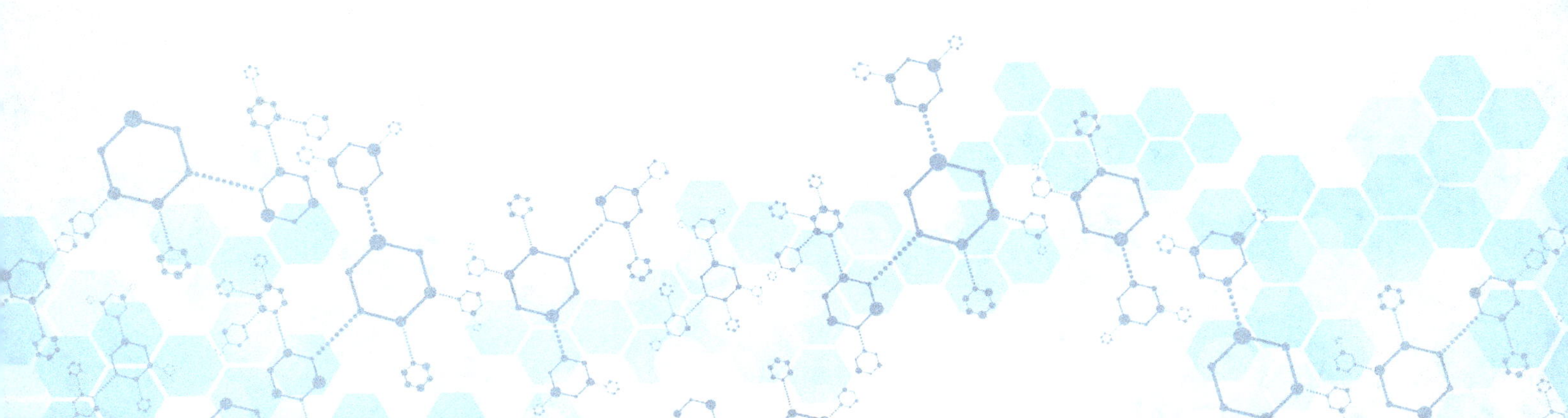

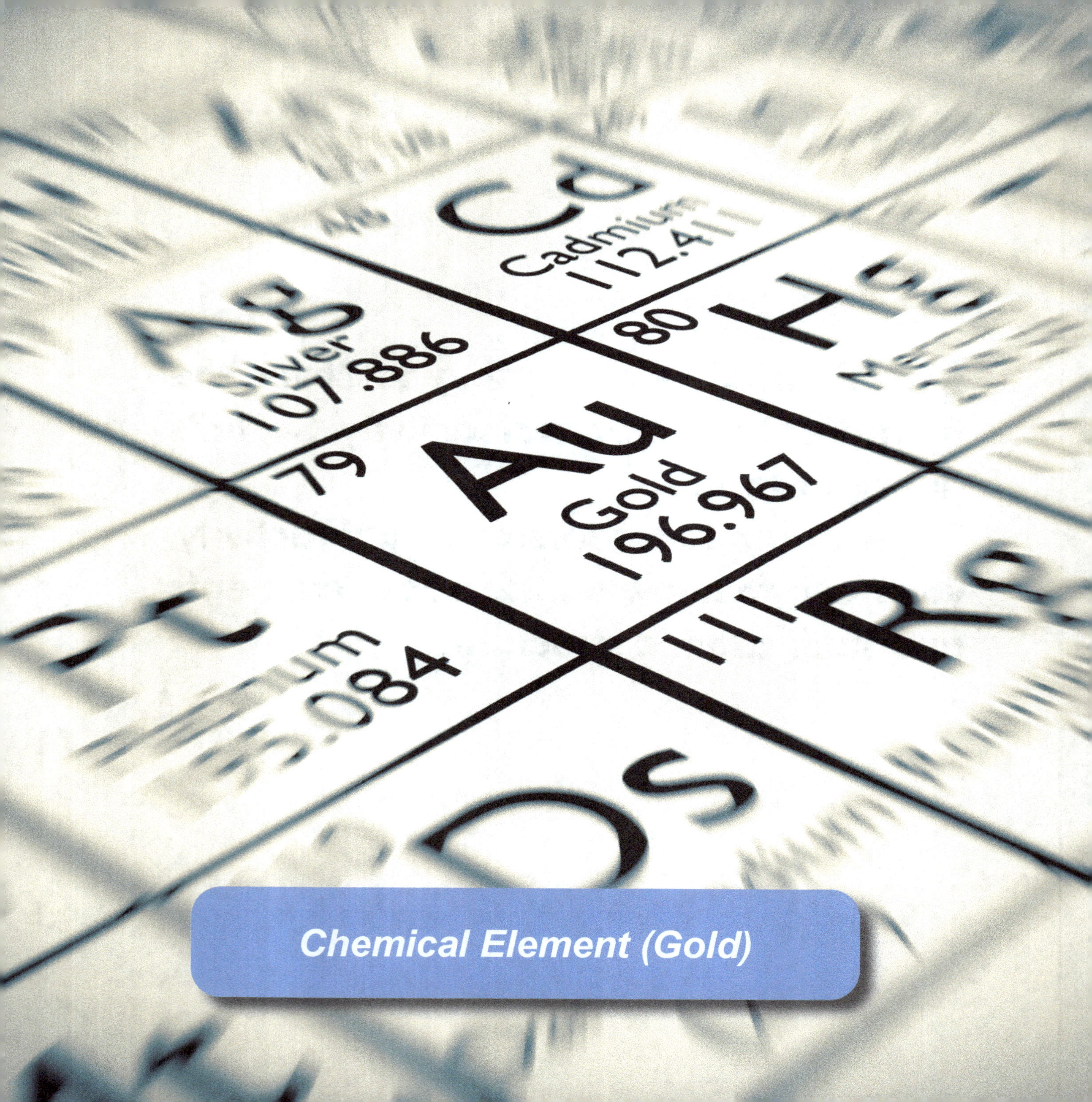

Chemical Element (Gold)

Each element has a unique atomic structure with a certain number of protons. This number is the atomic number of the element. The elements are arranged in the periodic table based on their atomic numbers. Each atom of an element has an equal number of protons and electrons.

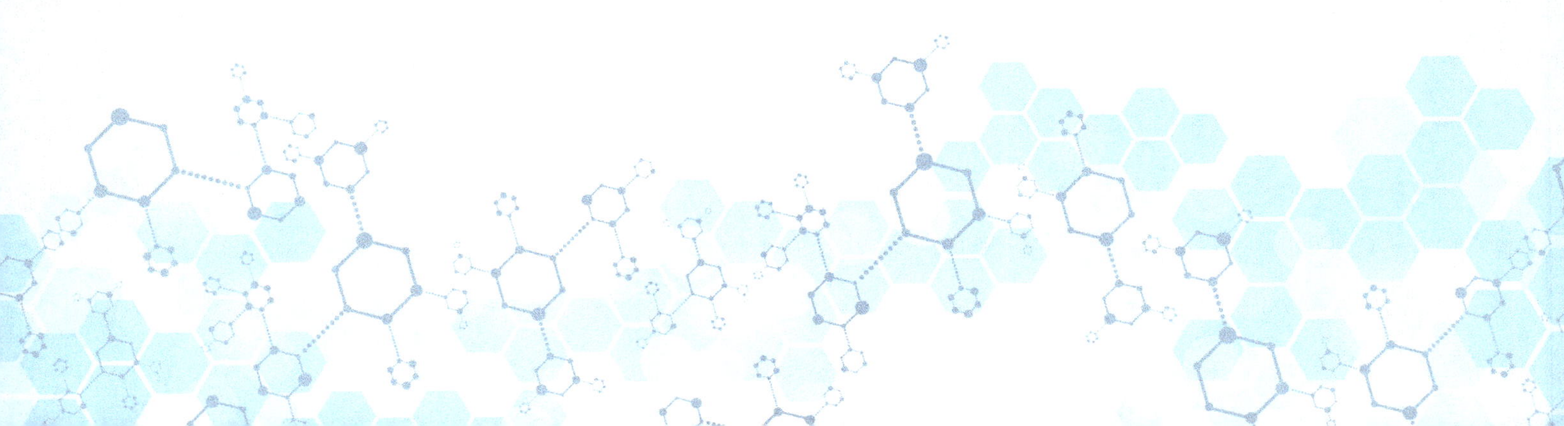

WHAT IS AN ISOTOPE?

Let's think about an atom of the element hydrogen. This atom has one proton and one electron and no neutrons. However, an isotope of hydrogen will have neutrons. The addition of these neutrons doesn't change the element.

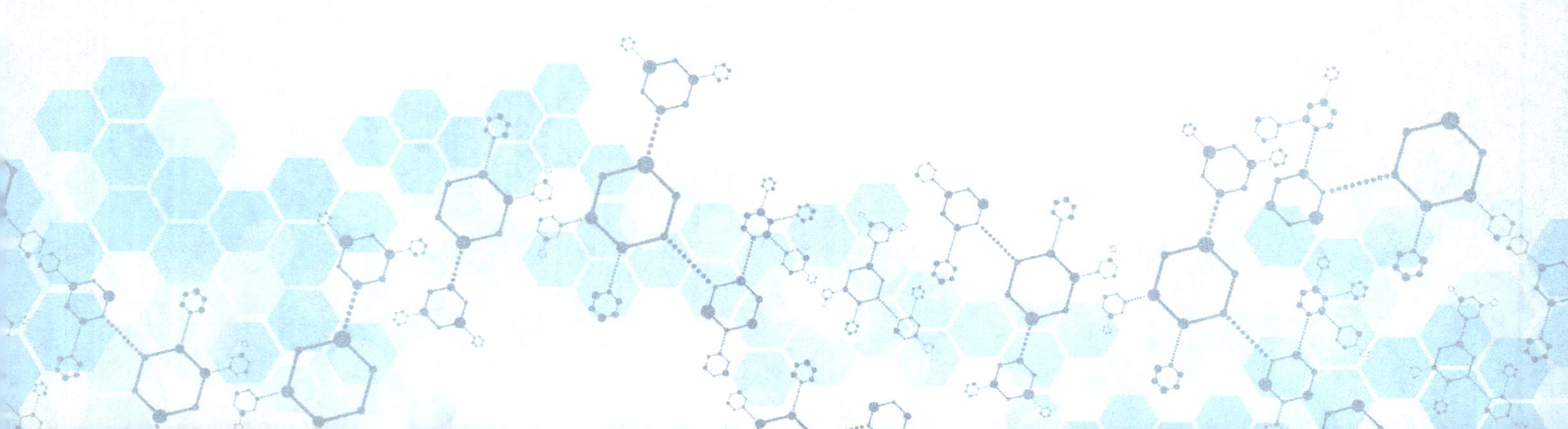

Chemical Element (Hydrogen)

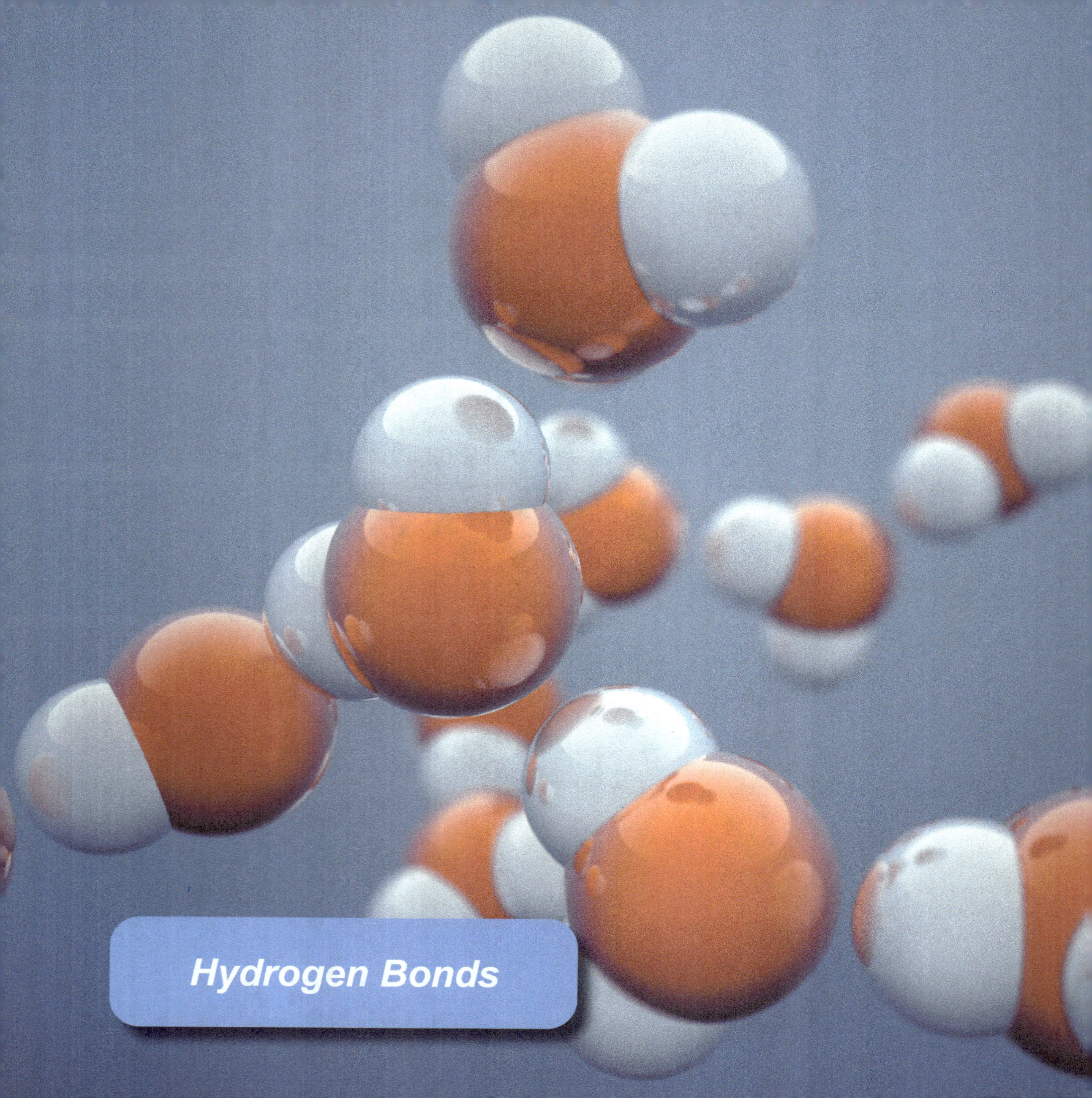
Hydrogen Bonds

The element is still hydrogen. Deuterium is an isotope of hydrogen that has one neutron and tritium is an isotope of hydrogen that has two neutrons. Isotopes are therefore atoms of a specific element that have different numbers of neutrons but the same number of protons and electrons.

HOW DO WE WRITE THE NAME OF AN ISOTOPE?

Hydrogen is actually the only element whose isotopes have names of their own. For the other elements, there are two ways the name can be written. For example, the isotope carbon-14 can be written as carbon-14 or also as 14C. Both of these methods use the mass of the atom.

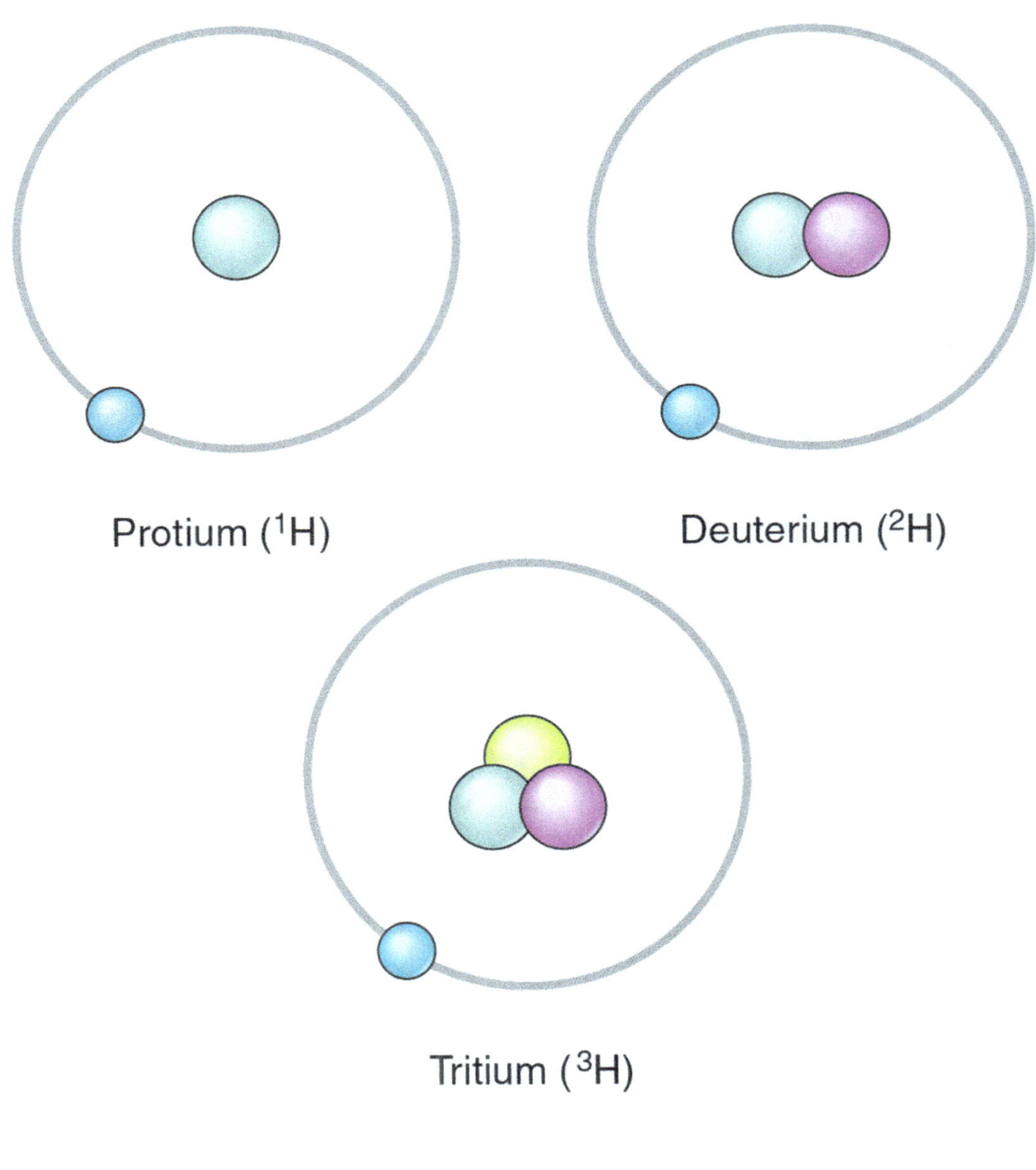

Protium (^{1}H)
Deuterium (^{2}H)
Tritium (^{3}H)
Hydrogen Isotopes

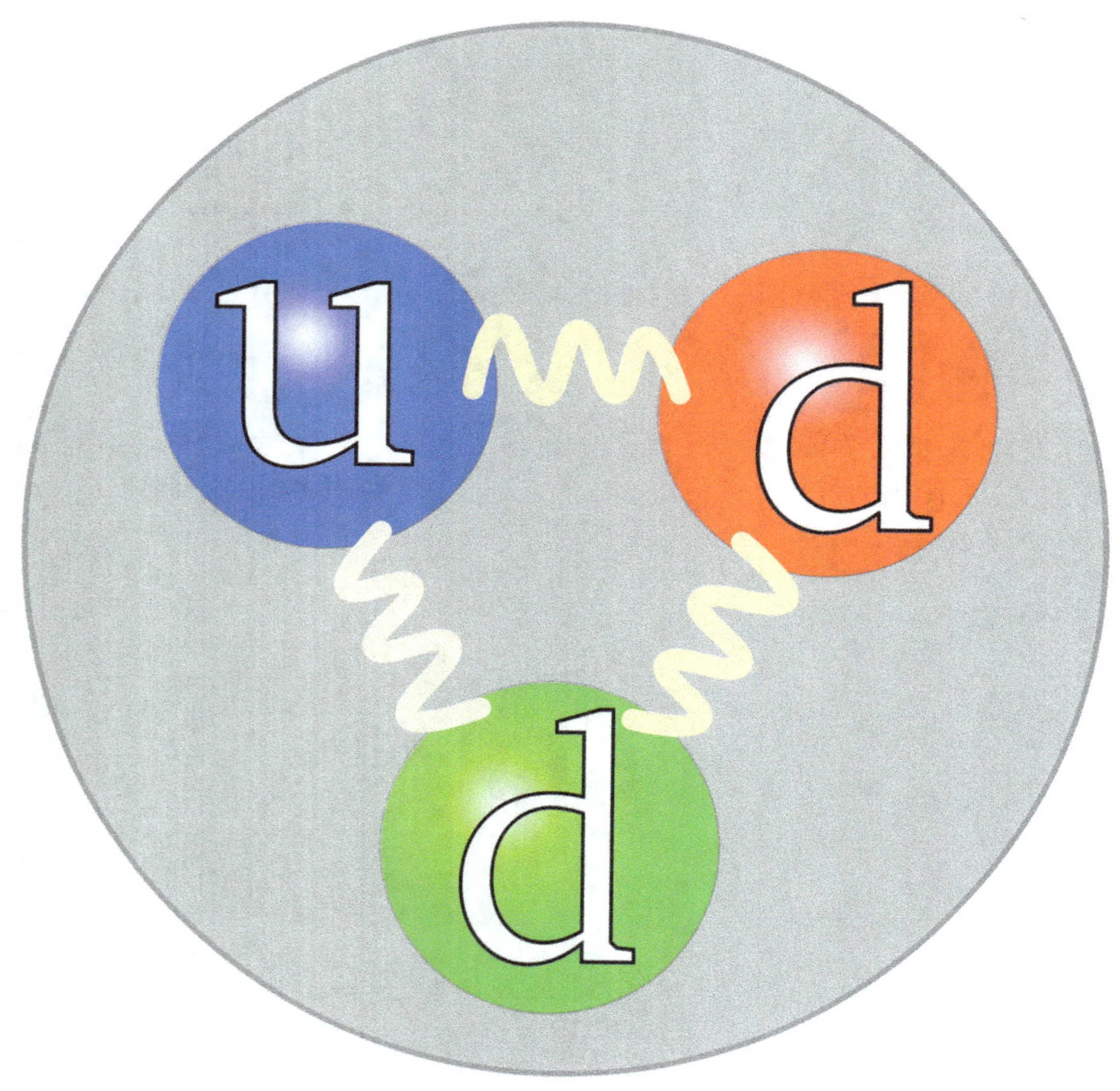

Neutron

The mass is the number of protons plus the number of neutrons. The number of protons in carbon is 6, so its isotope carbon-14 has 8 neutrons.

Neutrons don't have any electrical charge. That means that altering the number of neutrons in an element doesn't affect its chemistry. It does change its mass though and that is why isotopes are named by their mass.

STABLE AND UNSTABLE ISOTOPES

All elements have some isotopes. Hydrogen has the fewest number, xenon and cesium each have 36 isotopes. Some isotopes have a stable structure and others don't. If an isotope is unstable, eventually it will break down and decay. When this happens, it changes into another type of isotope or element.

Cesium crystals

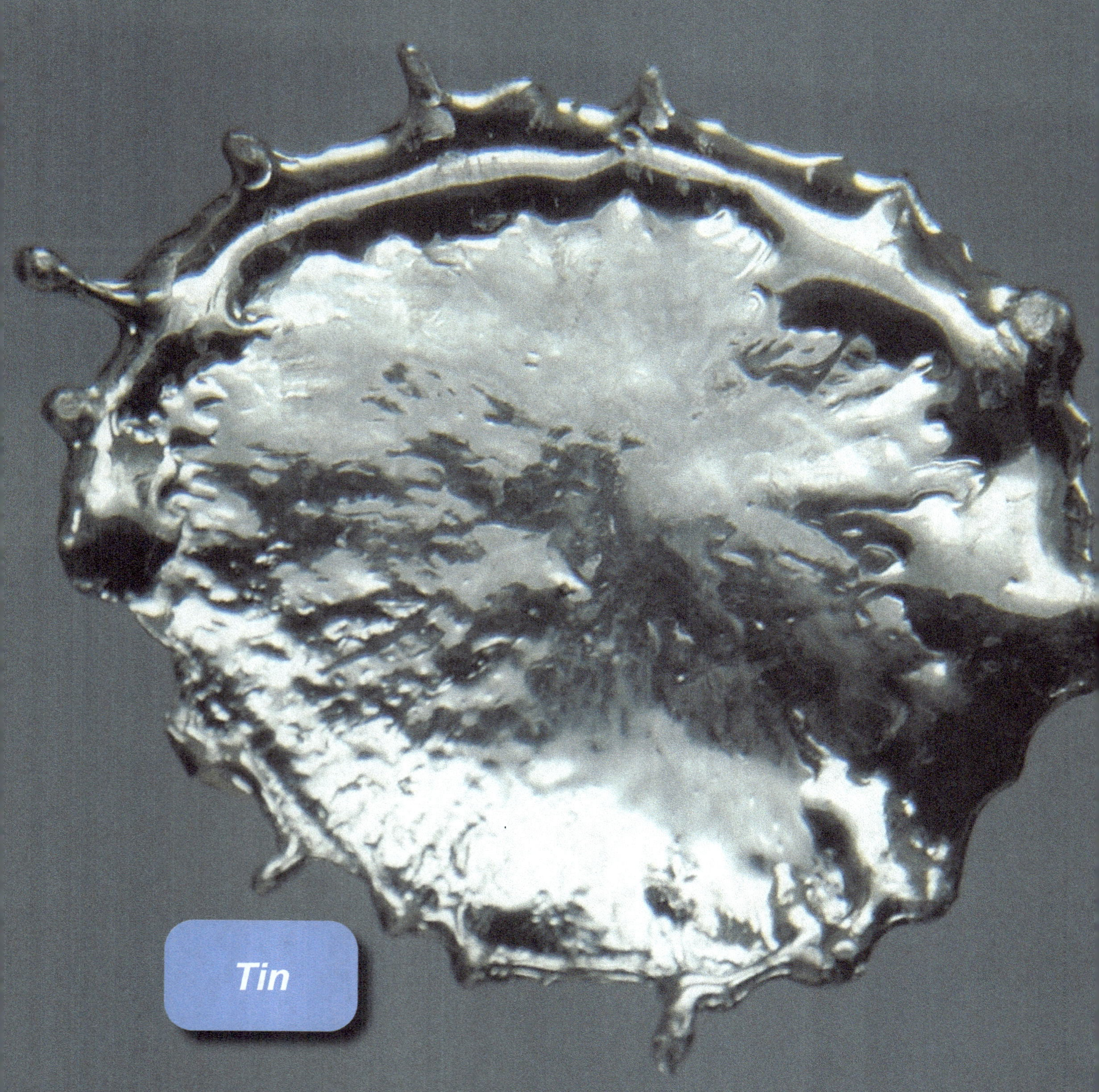
Tin

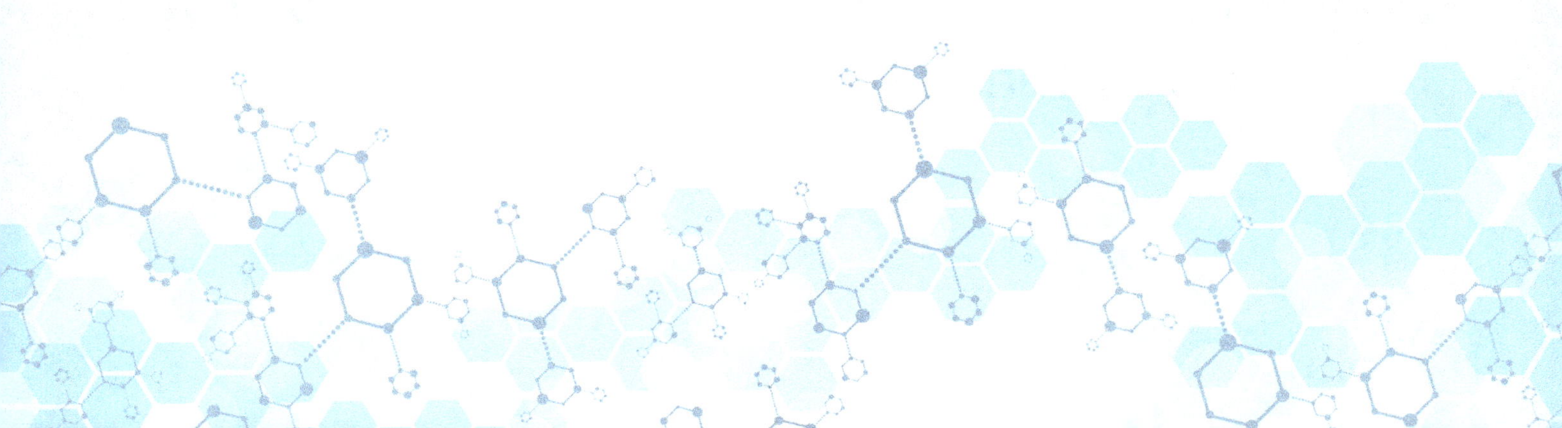

If an isotope is unstable, it's radioactive. In nature, most elements are composed of stable isotopes. Tin is the element with the most number of stable isotopes, a total of ten.

When an isotope is unstable, it gives out radiation, which is a form of energy. In other words, if there are an excess of neutrons compared with the number of protons, the isotope starts to eject particles until a stable nucleus happens. This process of radioactive decay can be categorized as three different types: alpha, beta, or gamma. Each unstable isotope will decay in one of these ways.

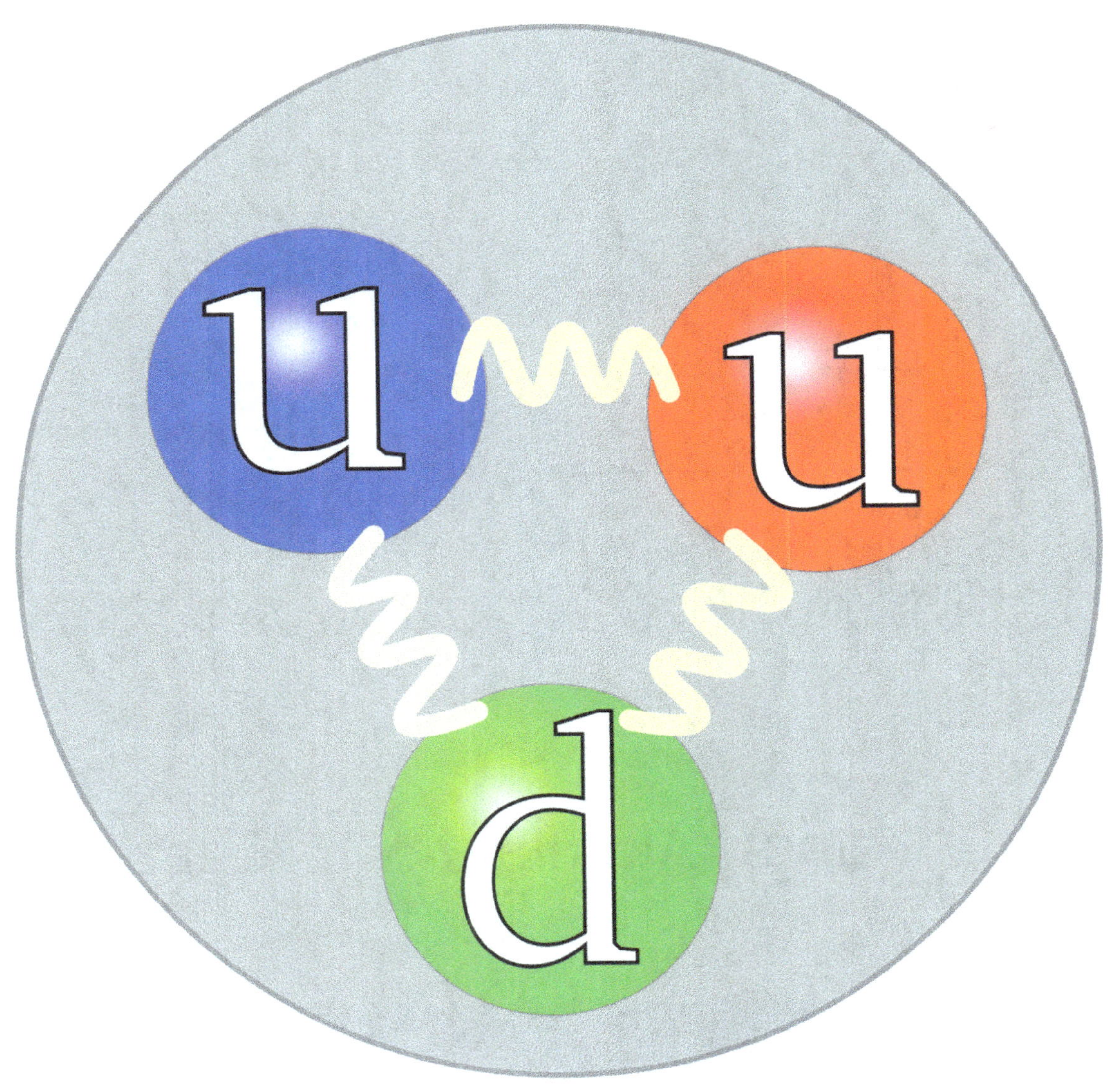

Proton

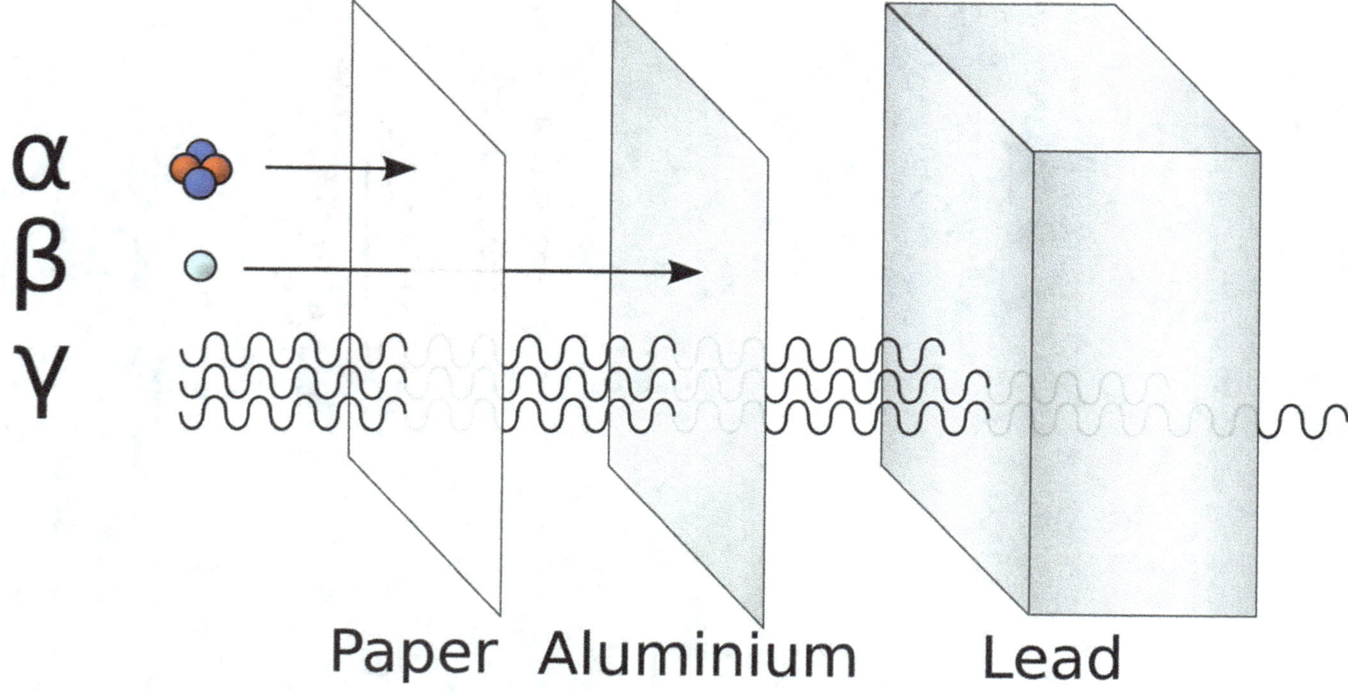

Alpha beta gamma radiation penetration

DIFFERENT TYPES OF RADIOACTIVITY

The different types of radioactivity are identified with Greek letters.

Alpha - Alpha particles are emitted when an isotope's nucleus has too many protons. Alpha particles are positively charged.

Beta - Beta particles are emitted when an isotope's nucleus has too many neutrons. Beta particles are negatively charged.

Gamma - Gamma particles are emitted when there is an excess of energy in the isotope's nucleus. Gamma particles don't have a charge.

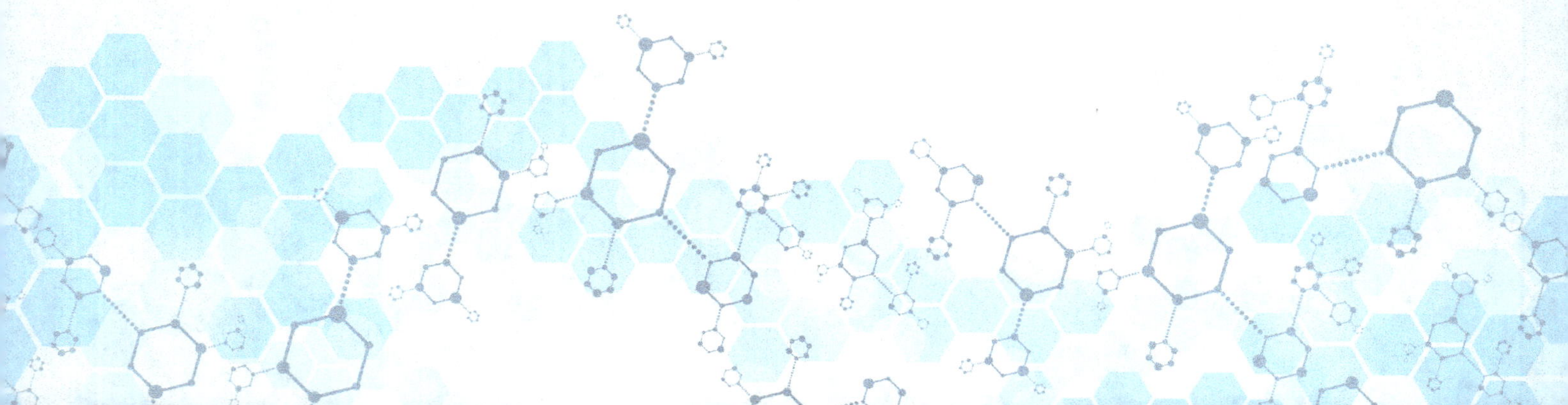

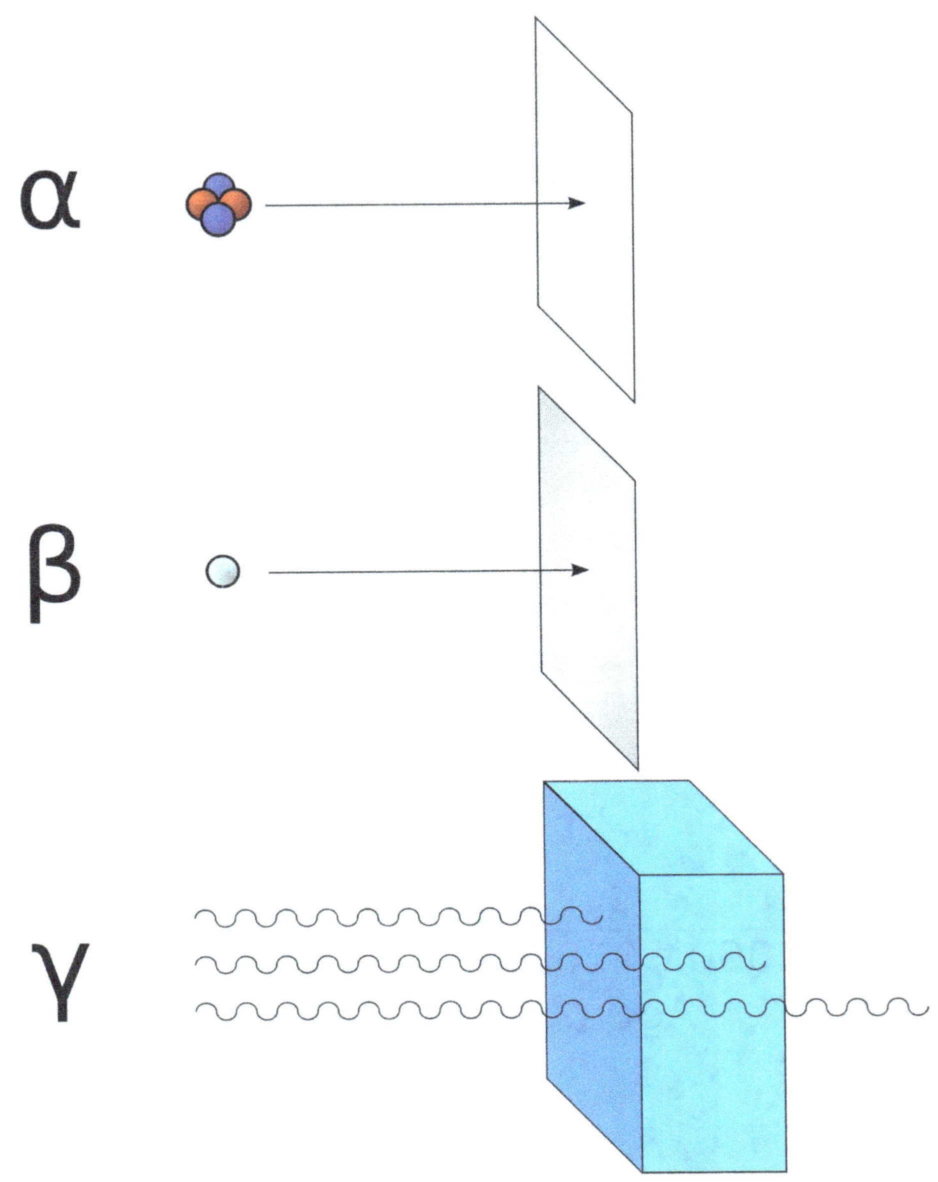

Alpha beta gamma radiation

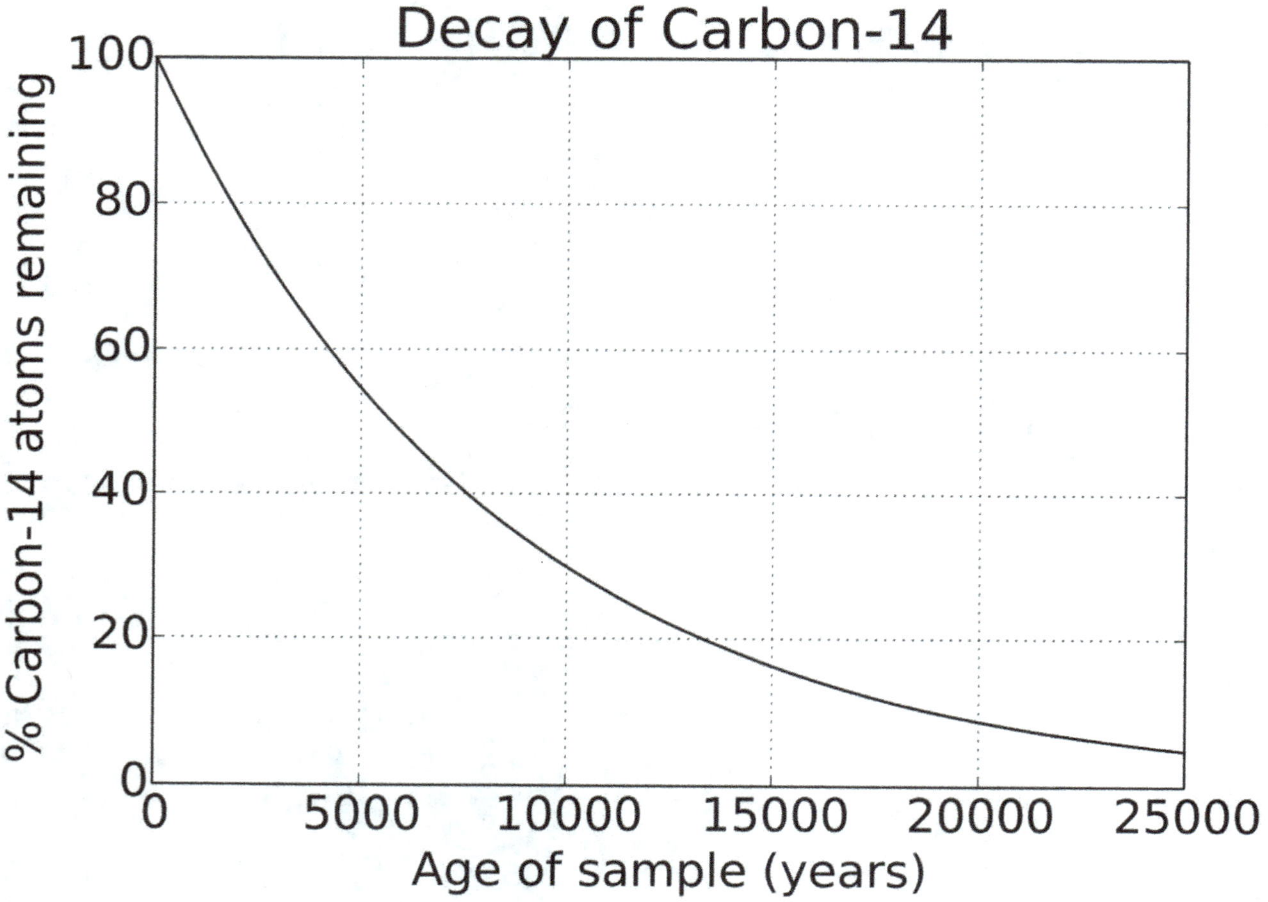

Radioactive decay of Carbon-14

HOW IS THE PROCESS OF RADIOACTIVITY MEASURED?

Some isotopes decay after a few seconds and others take thousands of years to decay! In order to express the process of radioactive decay, a unit of measurement was needed. The unit of measurement used is called the **curie** and is written as "Ci."

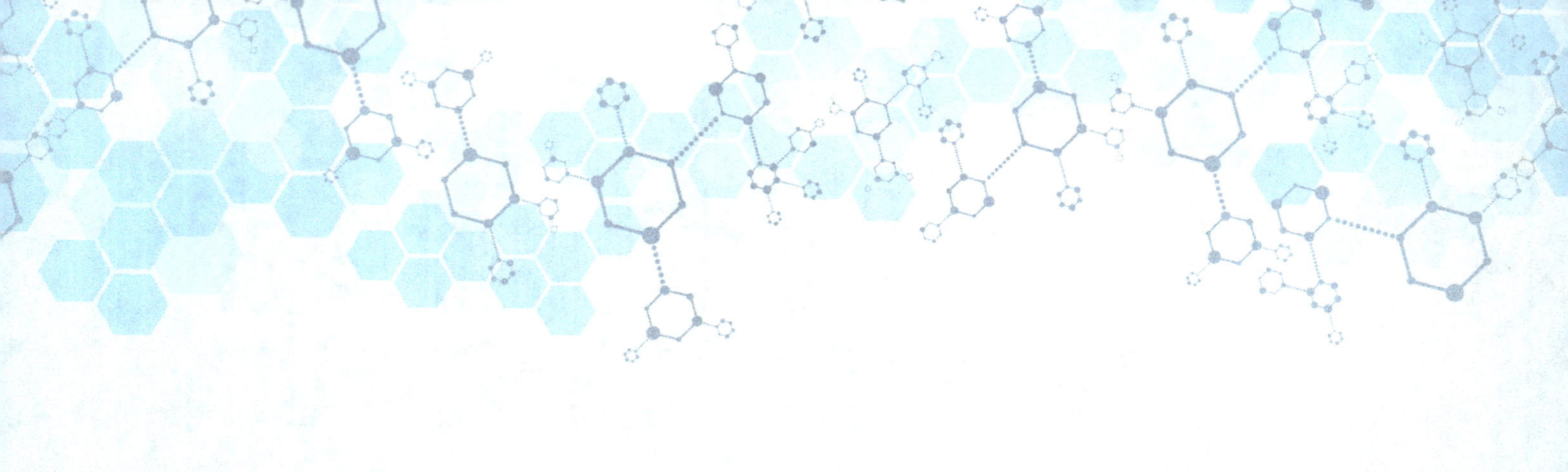

The curie was named after famous scientist Marie Curie who along with her husband discovered radium. The curie measures the number of atoms of an isotope that decay every second.

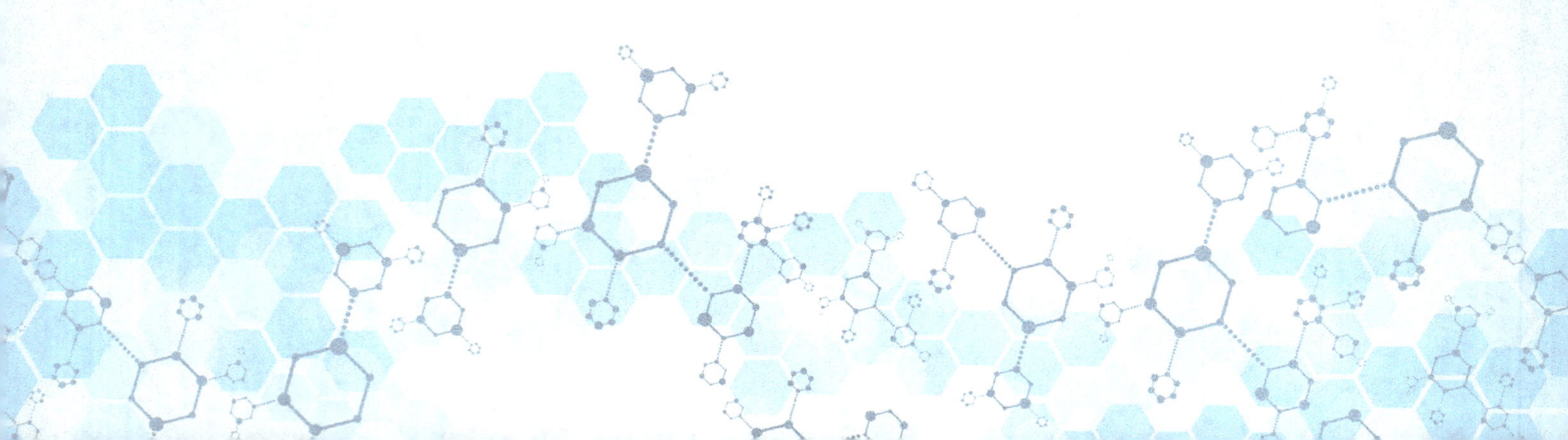

Marie Curie

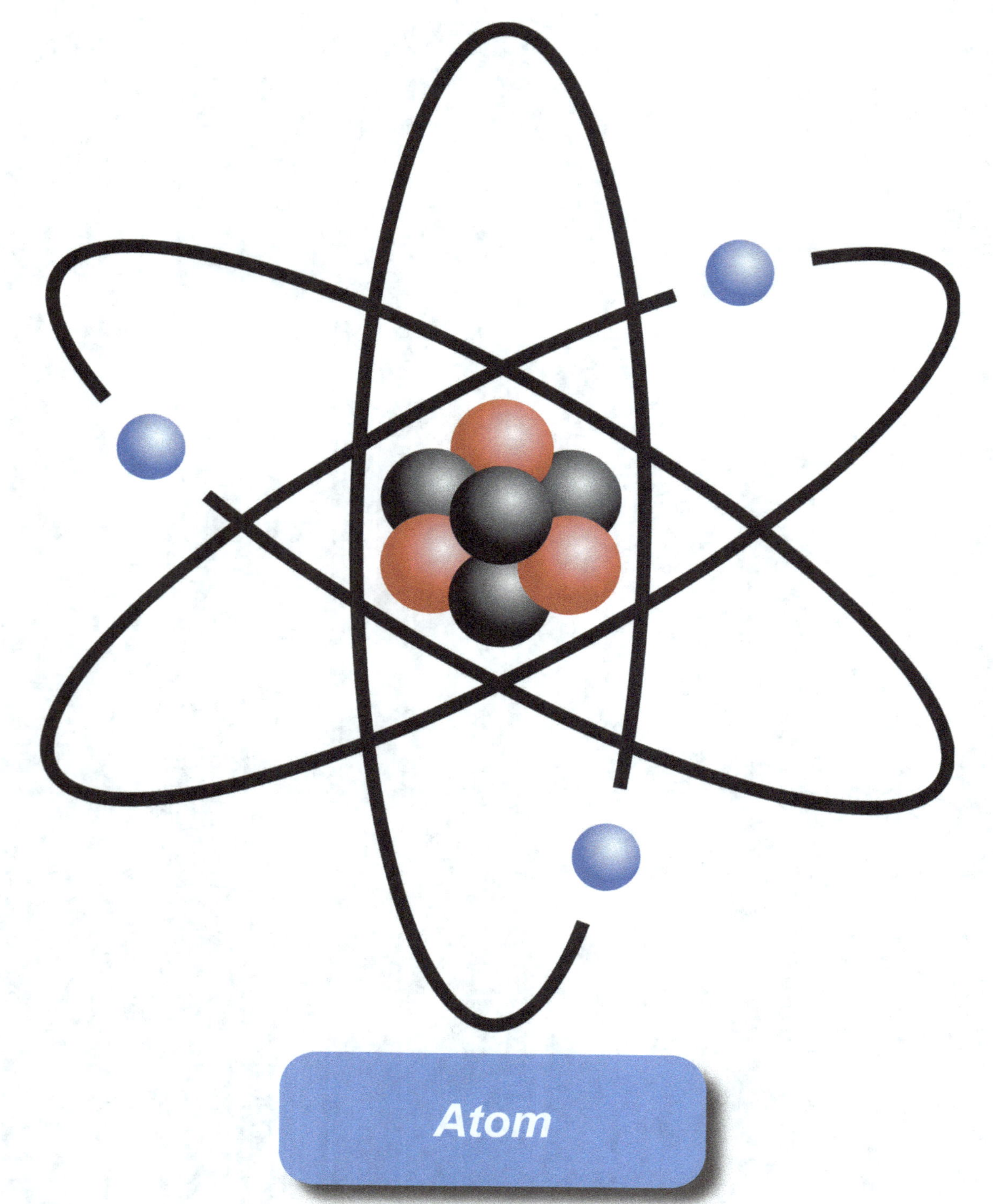

Atom

WHAT IS THE HALF-LIFE OF AN ISOTOPE?

The average time it takes for half the atoms in a specific isotope to undergo radioactive decay is called its half-life. For example, it takes 5,730 years for carbon-14 to reach its half-life. That means if you had a sample of the isotope with 500 atoms, you'd expect 250 of them to decay over the time span of 5,730 years.

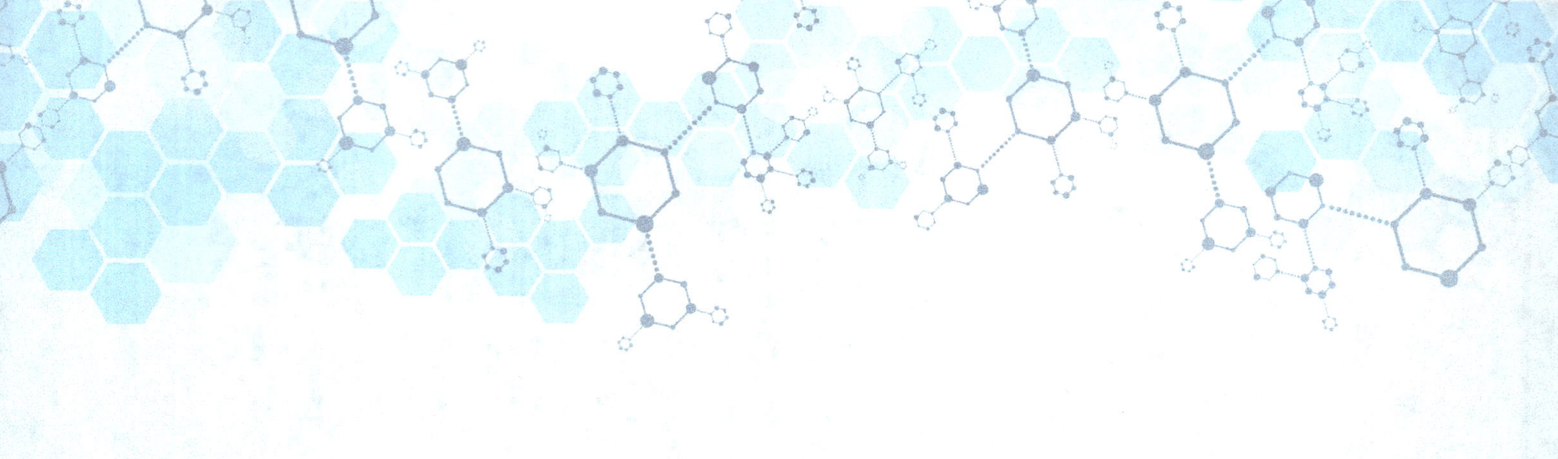

Some atoms will decay quickly and others won't for thousands of years. Of course, this figure is just based on an average. It's not a specific measurement for one sample, but instead it's an average based on the decay of billions of atoms.

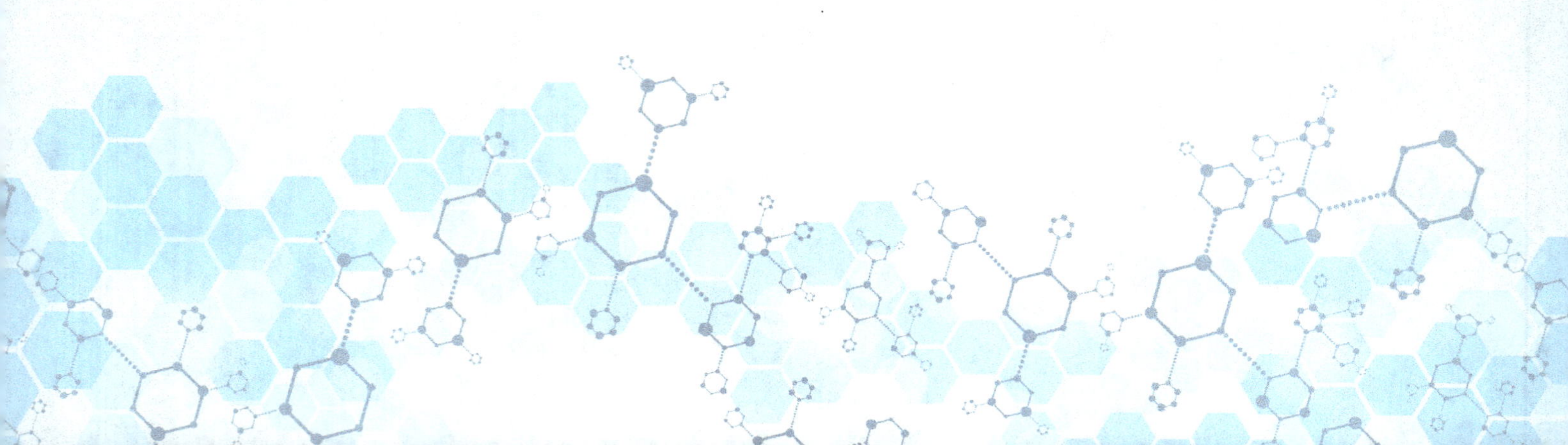

2068
Uranium-235 (Uranium Isotope)

A group of Archaeologists

WHY IS RADIOACTIVE HALF-LIFE IMPORTANT?

Knowledge about radioactive half-life is important because:

- ➜ It helps archaeologists date ancient artifacts. To determine the age of dead organic objects, scientists use the half-life of the isotope carbon-14. They calculate how much of the carbon-14 has changed and can use this measurement to tell the age of the substance.

- ⮕ It helps people working at facilities that create nuclear waste. It tells them how long they must store the waste until it is safe to dispose of. Some radioactive waste won't be safe until thousands of years go by.

- ⮕ It helps doctors to use safe radioactive tracers that are active enough to treat a patient's condition but decay fast enough that they don't hurt healthy cells.

A radioactive sample is considered safe after its radioactivity can't be measured. This happens at 10 half-lives.

Plutonium Isotopes

DECAYING TO OTHER ELEMENTS

During the process of decay, isotopes can lose some of their protons and electrons. When this happens, they become different elements. They sometimes change to other unstable elements and this can happen in a chain of radioactive events.

An example of this process is the isotope uranium-238. As it undergoes radioactive decay it changes to a long sequence of different elements and finally transforms into a stable isotope.

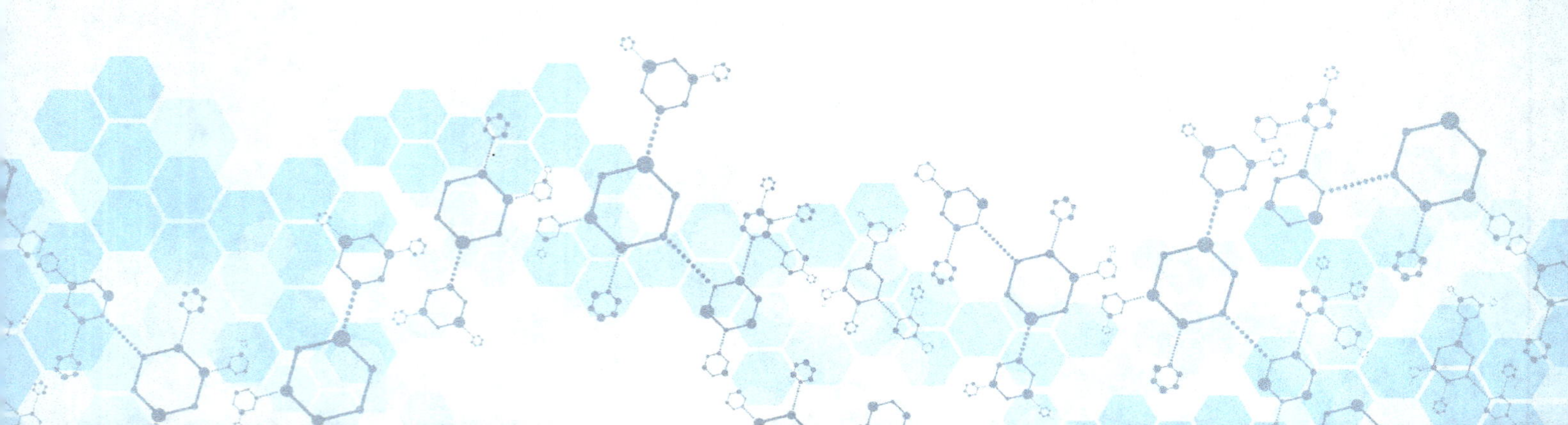

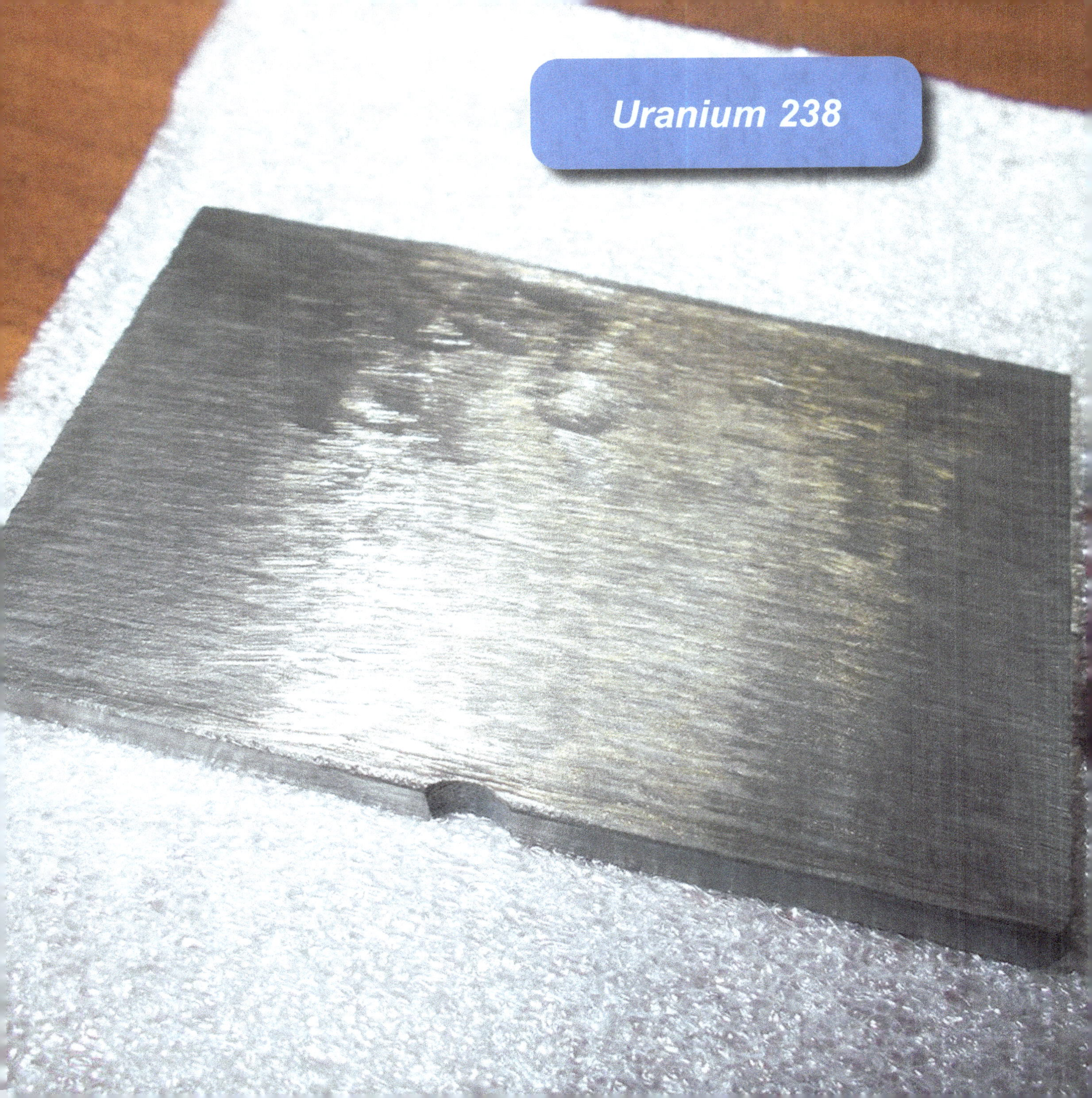

Uranium 238

Henri Becquerel

WHO DISCOVERED RADIOACTIVITY?

In 1896, the French scientist Henri Becquerel discovered radioactivity by accident when he was doing experiments to determine which materials were phosphorescent. Phosphorescent substances glow in the dark after they have been exposed to light. He thought that X-rays were somehow connected with phosphorescence.

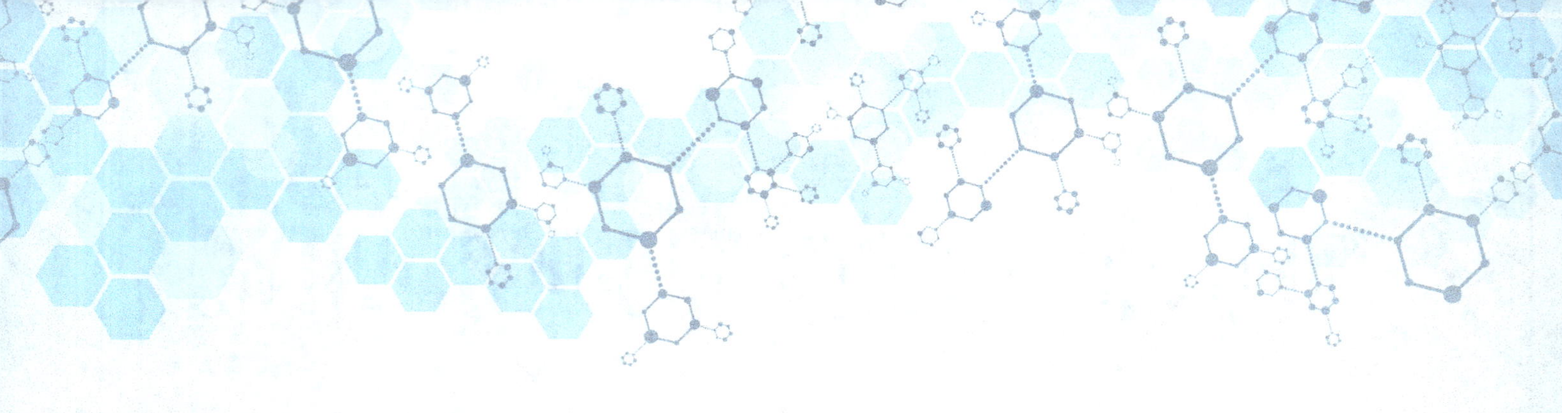

He wrapped a photographic plate in black paper. Then, he placed various minerals that were known to be phosphorescent on them. Nothing happened, except with uranium salts. These compounds blackened the plate. He soon found that this effect had nothing to do with phosphorescence, however.

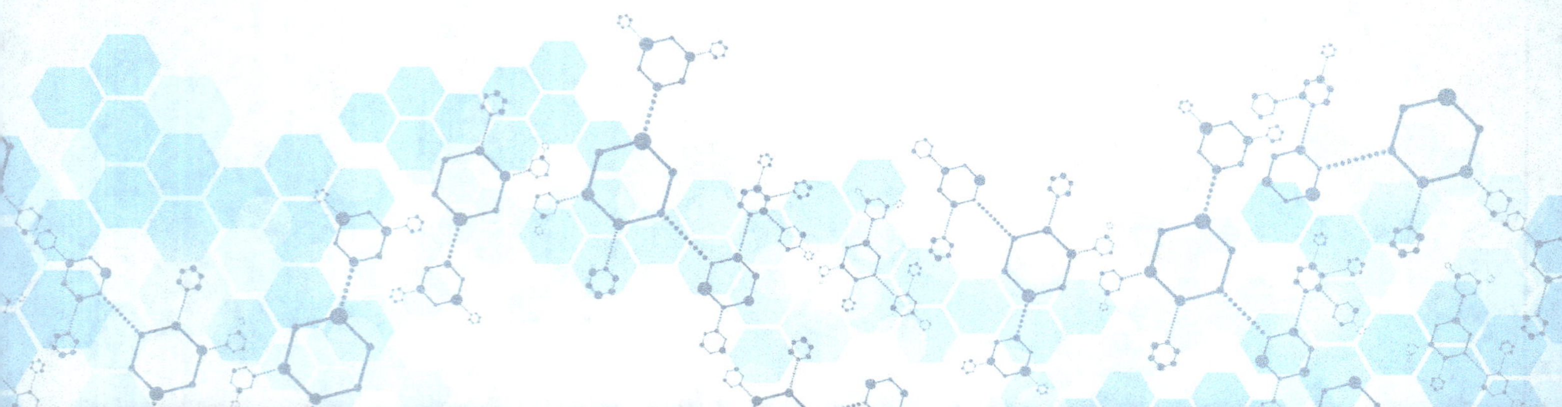

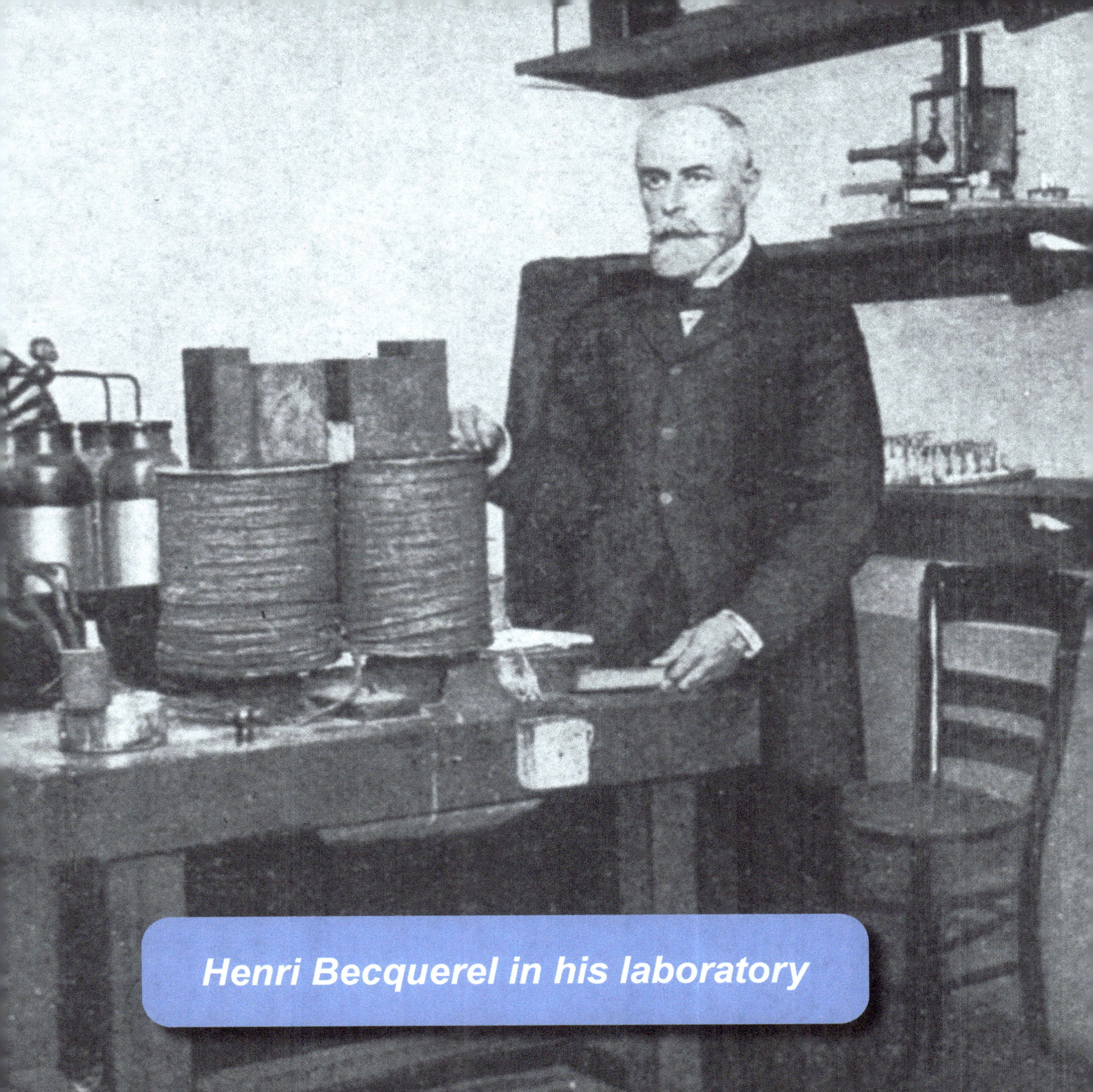

Henri Becquerel in his laboratory

Uranium

This happened even when the uranium salts had been kept in the dark and weren't exposed to light at all! At first, it appeared that the type of radiation the uranium compound was emitting was similar to X-rays. However, after further research, it was discovered that there were different types of radiation.

NATURAL AND MANMADE RADIATION

The Earth and all living things are constantly showered by radiation coming from space. Charged particles come into our atmosphere and magnetic field bringing both beta and gamma radiation. This radiation from space differs at varying locations throughout the world based on differences in both elevation and the magnetic field.

The soil, water, and plants around us all contain some level of radioactivity. Uranium and the elements it decays into, including radium and radon, are found all over the Earth. It's impossible to prevent exposure to radiation and still live on Earth. In addition to these sources, people are born with radioactive isotopes, such as potassium-40 and carbon-14 in their bodies.

Over 80% of the radiation exposure we have yearly is in the natural radiation just described, but there are also manmade exposures as well. The majority of the remaining 20% of the radiation exposure we get yearly is from X-rays as well as nuclear medicine and radiation therapy. There are also consumer products that expose us to some radiation risks, such as televisions, airport X-ray systems, and electron tubes.

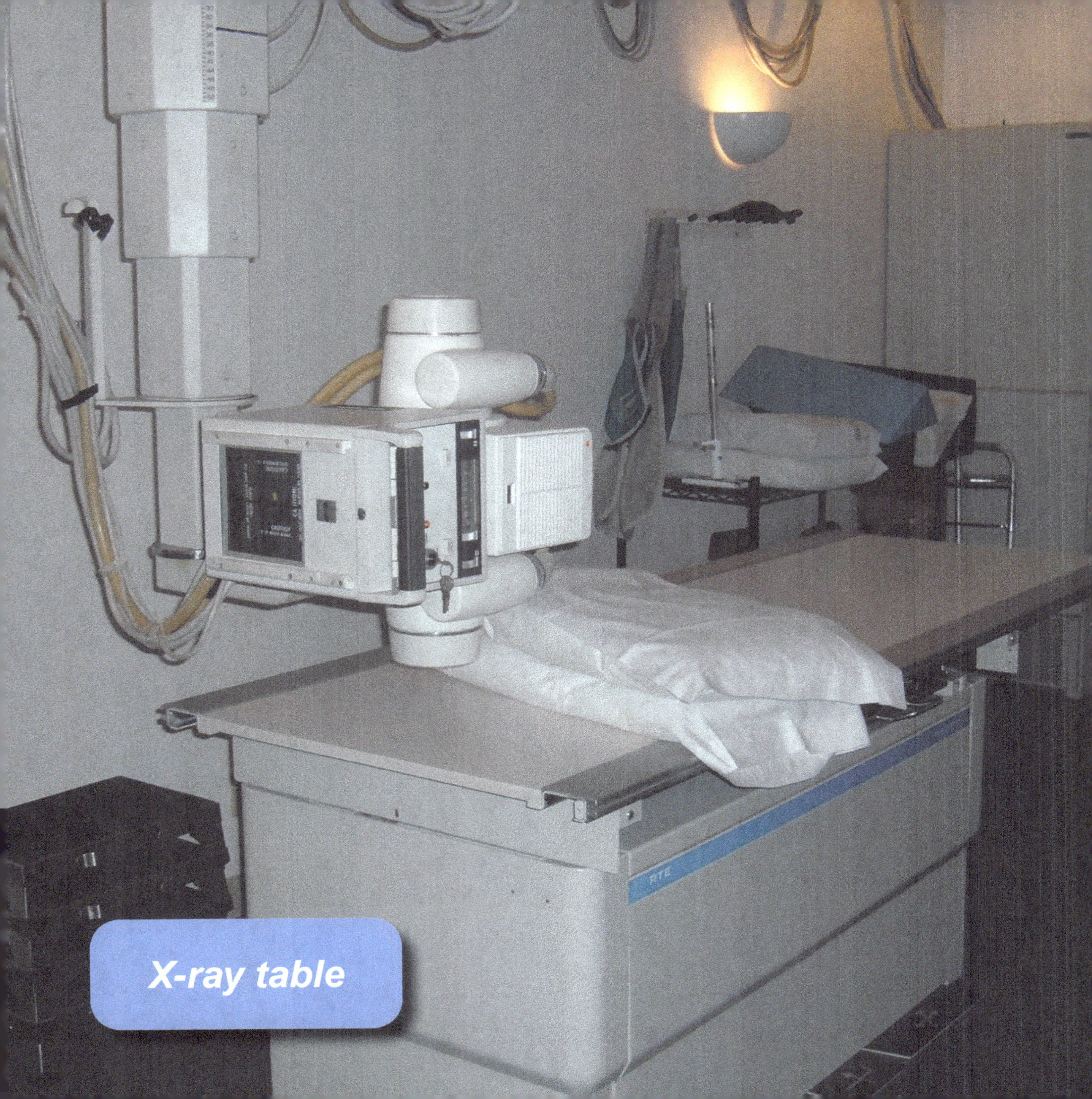
X-ray table

Chynobyl Nuclear Plant

There is always the danger of nuclear accidents from nuclear reactors as well. The long-term effects of these types of disasters occur over thousands of years. It's estimated that the city of Chernobyl, the site of a major nuclear disaster in 1986, will not be safe to inhabit for 20,000 more years. The explosion at Chernobyl emitted 400 times the radioactive material than the atomic bomb dropped on Hiroshima.

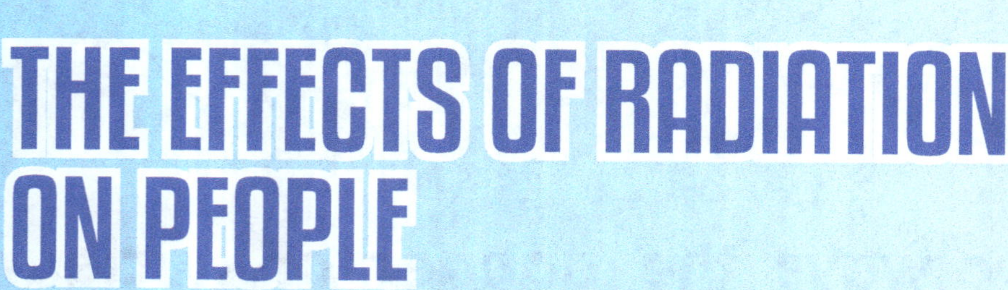

Many of the early scientists who worked with radiation died from its effects. At that time, the dangers of exposure to radiation weren't known. Exposure to radiation can change the structure of our cells. This causes mutations that sometimes produce cancer. The more exposure you have, the more dangerous it is.

Scanning for possible radiation exposure

Radiation hotspot in Japan

Most of the data we have about the correlation between radiation exposure and cancer comes from the survivors of the atomic bomb in Japan. Other data comes from patients who have had repeated diagnostic tests that exposed them to radiation. Although it's clear that radiation can cause many different types of cancer at high levels of exposure, the long-term effects of low-level exposure aren't yet fully known.

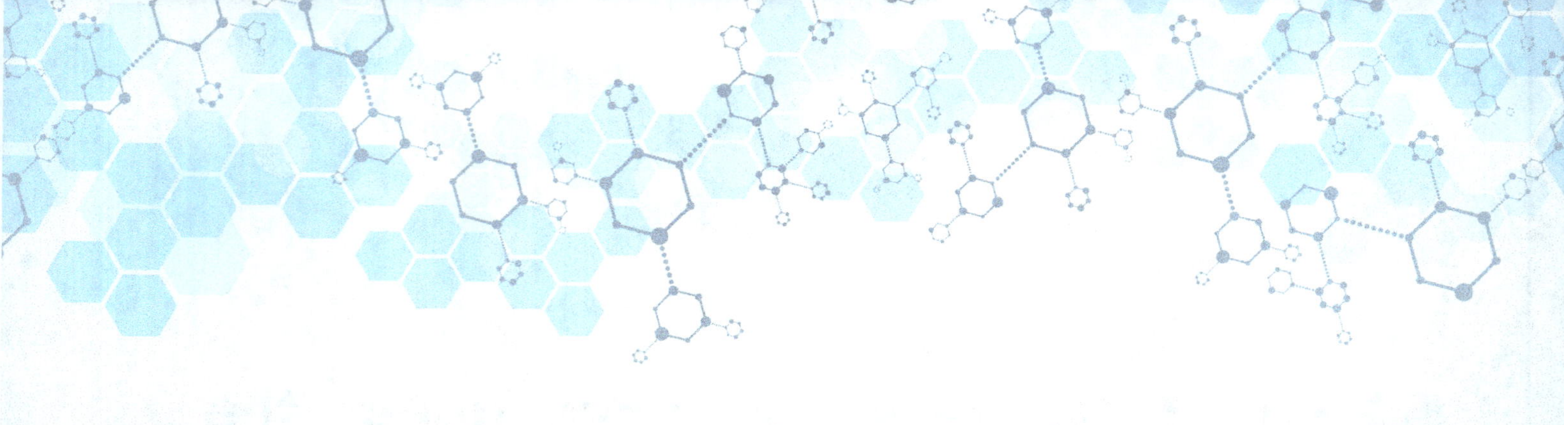

Despite the risks of radiation, radiation has some very useful applications in medicine, such as X-rays and radiation therapy, in the creation of energy, such as in nuclear power plants, and in archaeology, such as in carbon dating of artifacts.

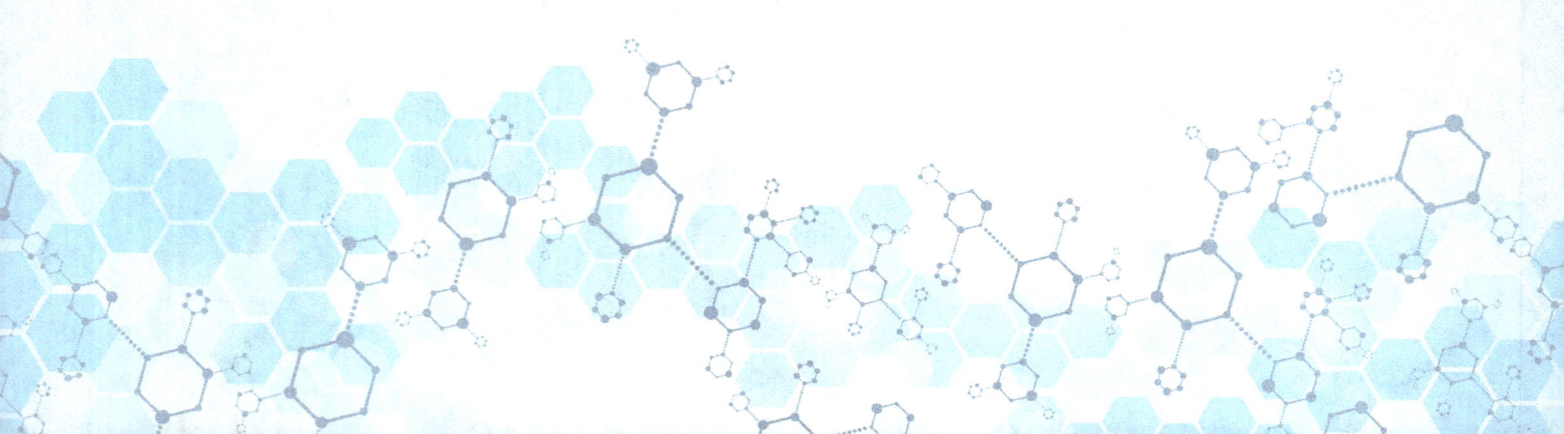

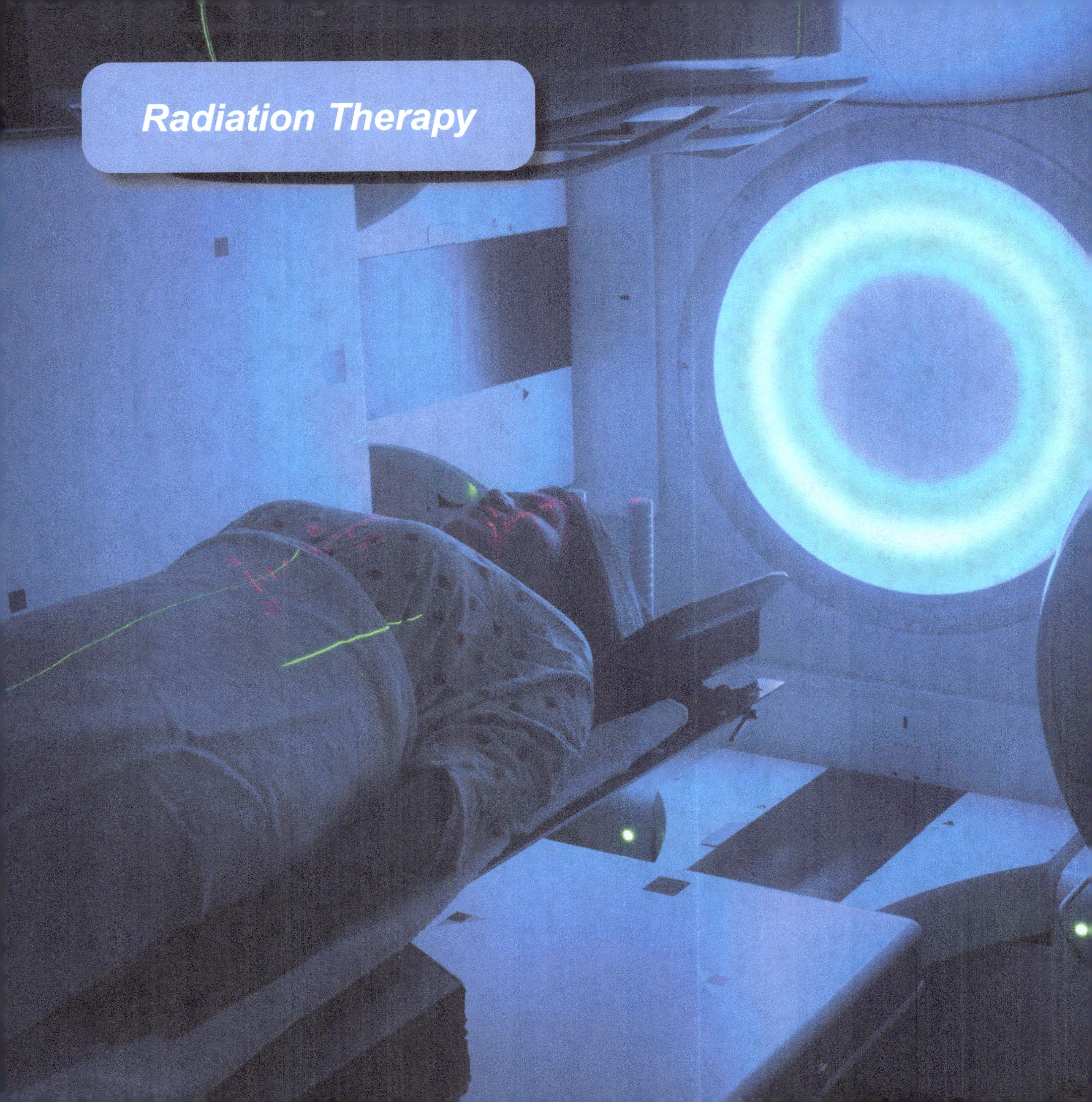

Radiation Therapy

Nuclear Power Plant

Awesome! Now you know more about the different types of radioactivity. You can find more Chemistry Books from Baby Professor by searching the website of your favorite book retailer.

Visit
BABY PROFESSOR
EDUCATION KIDS
www.BabyProfessorBooks.com
to download Free Baby Professor eBooks and view
our catalog of new and exciting Children's Books